WELCOME,
DOG LOVERS!

This book is dedicated to Boogie,
my teacher and muse.

DOGGIE LANGUAGE

Copyright © Lili Chin, 2020

Illustrations by Lili Chin

An Hachette UK Company
www.hachette.co.uk

Summersdale Publishers Ltd
Part of Octopus Publishing Group Limited
Carmelite House
50 Victoria Embankment
LONDON
EC4Y 0DZ
UK

www.summersdale.com

Printed and bound in Poland

ISBN: 978-1-78783-701-0

Substantial discounts on bulk quantities of Summersdale books are available to corporations, professional associations and other organizations. For details contact general enquiries: telephone: +44 (0) 1243 771107 or email: enquiries@summersdale.com.

DOGGIE
Language

WRITTEN AND ILLUSTRATED BY
LILI CHIN

summersdale

Many years ago, I was watching a video of myself training my dog, Boogie. I had seen this video several times before, but this time I noticed Boogie yawn and lick his lip after I tugged on his collar. In my earlier viewings, I was so focused on how well Boogie was responding to "Sit" that I had completely missed these signals.

Having just read Turid Rugaas' *On Talking Terms With Dogs*, this time I noticed and understood that the "yawn" and "lip lick" were signs of discomfort, and that these were Boogie's responses to the collar pressure on his neck. This was a mind-blowing realization for me, and from then on, I could never unsee these signals again.

I was determined to learn more about dog body language to become a better human to my dog. Amazed that this information wasn't better known in popular culture, I used my illustrations to share what I was learning with other dog lovers.

Over the past decade of my career, I have had the privilege of creating dog body language images for many dog-training professionals and welfare groups. My illustrations have appeared in "dog-bite prevention" campaigns, training books and museum exhibitions. My Doggie Language poster has been translated into many languages and used by rescues and shelters around the world. The important shared message: by learning dog body language, we can become more responsible guardians and caregivers. We can avoid causing harm to our companion animals and know when they need help.

Science confirms that dogs are thinking, feeling, social individuals. Like humans, dogs feel fear, anger,

happiness, sadness and surprise. They have likes and dislikes. They can feel confused or conflicted, and when they socialize, they do their best to maintain the peace and avoid conflict. Just like us.

Humans differ from dogs in that we like to communicate with physical touch (hugging, shaking hands) and making direct eye contact. What might surprise many people is that dogs are communicating visually all the time. They do not need to bark or physically touch to let each other – and us – know what they dislike, what they are comfortable with and what they absolutely enjoy.

When a dog tells us something is too intense for them (too close, too loud, too direct, too much movement or too weird) we may unintentionally make the situation worse if we misread their body language and add to their stress. A dog who growls, bites or starts a fight usually does so as a last resort when all their smaller communication signals have had no effect.

Thankfully, the times they are a-changin', and dog lovers around the world are becoming more knowledgeable about dog body language, and how to be more empathic listeners and communicators. I hope this book will contribute to that self-education. When we stop bossing our dogs around and instead show them that we see and respect their signals – the way that polite and friendly dogs do – we create a dialogue that dogs really like!

It is hard to put all the nuances of a dog's body language into words, so the drawings in this book are designed to help you know what to look for, and to make distinctions between similar expressions. As you compare drawings, you will see key differences that give you a context to take into consideration. For example, a panting mouth that looks like it is "smiling" may in fact signal anxiety if you also notice the big pupils, wrinkled forehead, pinned-back ears and "spatula tongue".

Even if your dog doesn't look like any of the dogs I have drawn (there are, after all, over 400 different dog breeds and physical types in the world), the drawings should still help you recognize these signals in your own dog.

I truly believe that the more we understand what we are seeing, the more we will learn to see, and the more we practise observing and "listening" to our best friends, the better we will be able to help them feel safe, confident and happy.

Lili

REMEMBER:

Look at the whole body

Always look at the dog's whole body in addition to single body parts. What does the dog's overall posture and movement look like?

Feelings are contextual

While a dog's body language tells us what they are feeling, we don't have the full picture without considering the context. What is going on? How is the dog's body language changing in relation to what is happening?

Every dog is an individual

A dog's expressiveness is also dependent on their age, health, breed, physical type and unique past experiences. A puppy's communication style will be different from that of an adult dog. It is normal for different dogs to respond differently to the same situation.

1. ALWAYS LOOK AT MY WHOLE BODY

2. ALWAYS LOOK AT THE CONTEXT

3. EVERY DOG IS AN INDIVIDUAL

CONTENTS

How a dog might respond to a friend – old or new.

GREETING STRETCH

Visual signs:

- Slow stretch, on the ground or up onto a person
- Soft eyes, soft ears

What your dog may be feeling:

- Happy

HAPPY HELLO

Visual signs:

- Relaxed face and body
- No tension in movements
- Bouncy gait
- Wiggly butt, wide wags

What your dog may be feeling:

- Interested
- All kinds of happy
- "Hello, friend!"
- "I am SO happy I have to pick up my toy!"

HEAD TILT

Visual signs:

- Head tilted to one side
- Ears forward
- Eyes attentive

What your dog may be feeling:

- Interested
- Curious or surprised
- "Huh?"

GREETINGS

BUTT SNIFF

Visual signs:

- Nose to butt

What your dog may be feeling:

- Curious
- Needing to get information
- If butt sniffs are brief and dogs move around freely, this is a friendly greeting. (A prolonged sniff may be impolite.)
- Each individual dog's body language will tell you how the interaction is going.

FRIENDLY NOSE TOUCH

Visual signs:

- Approaching from the side or in a curve (instead of making a beeline)
- Soft eyes, soft ears
- Nose to nose
- Relaxed bodies

What your dog may be feeling:

- Curious
- Comfortable
- "How are you?"

EYES

We have trained dogs to look at us directly, but in the dog world, indirect eye contact is actually more polite.

SOFT EYES

Visual signs:

- Almond-shaped
- No direct eye contact
- Relaxed ears, mouth, body

What your dog may be feeling:

- Happy, peaceful
- Non-confrontational

HARD STARE OR GLARING

Visual signs:

- Sustained direct eye contact
- Forward ears, tight mouth
- Stiffness or stillness

What your dog may be feeling:

- Concerned or annoyed
- Confrontational
- Glaring can be a part of Stalking (see p.38)

SOFT EYES
NO DIRECT EYE CONTACT

RELAXED EARS

HAPPY MOUTH

RELAXED MUSCLES

TARGET LOCKED

HARD STARE
MORE THAN TWO SECONDS

STILLNESS, TENSION

LIPS FORWARD, CLOSED MOUTH

EYES

PUPPY EYES
OR "INNER EYEBROW RAISE"

Visual signs:

- Sustained eye contact
- Eyebrows raised
- Forward ears

What your dog may be feeling:

- "When I do this, I get..."
- "When I do this, my human…"
- Although sustained staring is not polite in the dog world, in our world dogs learn that eye contact can get humans to do things.
- Often misinterpreted as "guilty" or "starving"

BLINKING EYES

Visual signs:

- Squinting or blinking
- Avoiding direct eye contact

What your dog may be feeling:

- Uncomfortable, when something or someone is too intense
- "Please take it easy."
- Frequent blinking may mean more discomfort. When the dog is leaning away, there is possibly pain.

EYES

"WHALE EYE"

Visual signs:

- Big, dilated pupils, whites showing
- Eyes are focused in the opposite direction to where the dog's head is pointing
- Body is frozen or not moving

What your dog may be feeling:

- Conflicted or trapped
- Fight or flight?
- "How do I escape?"
- "Please give me space!"

DIFFERENT TYPES OF EYES

Some dog breeds have larger, rounder eyes or wrinkled brows and they could look like they are staring or stressed when they are not.

If a dog's eyes are hard for us to see because they are too small or covered under fur or wrinkles, it's all the more important to look at the whole body!

POSTURE

We can tell a lot about a dog's mood by changes in their overall body posture and movement.

RELAXED, HAPPY-GO-LUCKY

Visual signs:

- No tension in face and body
- Balanced weight
- Easy movements

What your dog may be feeling:

- Happy-go-lucky
- Enjoying their environment
- Not focused on anything in particular
- Just hanging out

POSTURE

ALERT, INTERESTED

Visual signs:

- Ears move forward and up
- Head and body lean forward
- Tail moves up

What your dog may be feeling:

- Interested
- Surprised
- Curious
- Something has changed in their environment.
- Other body language details will indicate whether this is curiosity or concern.

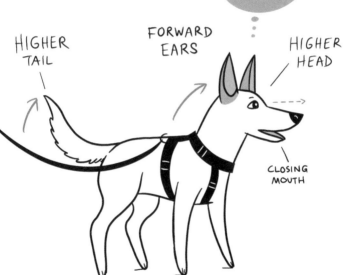

POSTURE

STALKING

Visual signs:

- Head and chest are lowered
- Ears move forward
- Eyes are staring
- Whole body is creeping forward

What your dog may be feeling:

- Very focused
- Prepared to chase
- "I'm gonna get you!"
- Stalking is a natural dog behaviour that, depending on context, can be deadly serious or a part of play.
- For some herding dogs, stalking is part of their job.

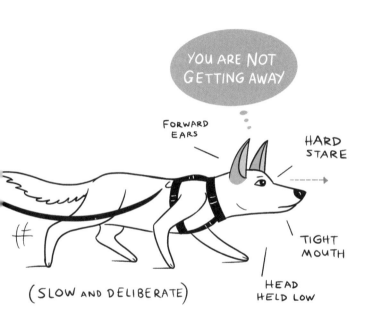

POSTURE

UNSURE

Visual signs:

- Front end is leaning forward while weight is still on the back end
- Head and ears are lowered

What your dog may be feeling:

- Unsure
- Cautious
- Conflicted: approach or retreat?
- Needing to get more information
- Ready to escape
- "Am I safe?"
- Other body language details can indicate whether this is curiosity or anxiety.

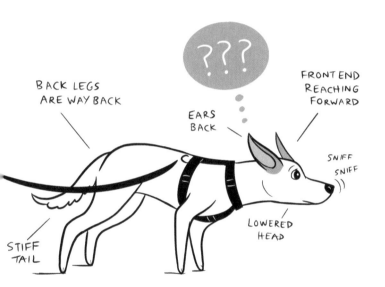

POSTURE

ANXIOUS, SCARED

Visual signs:

- Cowering or leaning away
- Head is lowered
- Ears are pinned back
- Tail is low or tucked down
- Body is still or frozen
- Possible shivering (when not cold)

What your dog may be feeling:

- Very unsafe
- Overwhelmed with fear
- Wanting to avoid interaction

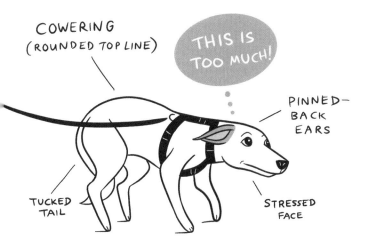

SUSPICIOUS, THREATENING

Visual signs:

- Standing tall and leaning forward
- Eyes are staring
- Ears are forward
- Tightly closed mouth
- Tail is high and stiff

What your dog may be feeling:

- Very annoyed
- Tense and purposeful
- Ready to fight
- "This is a warning."
- "I could hurt you."

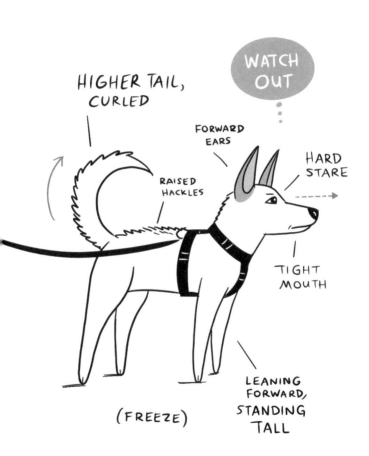

POSTURE

THREATENED, DEFENSIVE

Visual signs:

- Body is cowering or leaning back
- Tail is low or tucked
- Mouth is snarling, teeth showing
- Ears pinned back

What your dog may be feeling:

- Terrified, defensive
- Trapped
- Ready for fight or flight
- "Don't make me hurt you!"

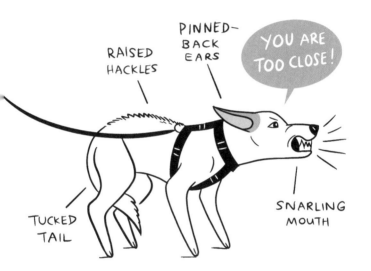

ANGRY, EXPLOSIVE

Visual signs:

- Lunging forward
- Mouth is snarling, teeth showing
- Hackles may be raised

What your dog may be feeling:

- Angry
- Extremely stressed
- Offence is the best defence!

Usually, this is a last resort when other signals have been ignored and the stressful situation has not changed.

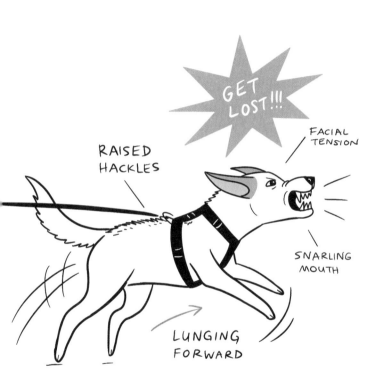

FRANTIC

Often misinterpreted as "happy!"

Visual signs:

- Jumping up on someone
- Pulling toward something
- Mouth anxious, panting or barking (see p.54)
- Facial tension

What your dog may be feeling:

- Overwhelmed and frustrated
- "I need to get closer!"
- "I need to leave!"

MOUTHS

Dogs' mouths are frequently misinterpreted,
perhaps because we are distracted by their teeth.
Here are some tips!

HAPPY, SMILING MOUTH

Visual signs:

- Can be open or softly closed
- Tongue is resting or relaxed
- Soft eyes, relaxed ears
- Smooth forehead

What your dog may be feeling:

- Relaxed
- Happy

RELAXED EARS

SMOOTH FOREHEAD

SOFT EYES

TONGUE IS RESTING

RELAXED TONGUE

MOUTHS

ANXIOUS MOUTH

Can be confused with a happy mouth!

Visual signs:

- Mouth can be open or closed
- Lip corners are stretched back in a grimace
- Tongue is wide and scooped
- May be panting
- Face and body are tense

What your dog may be feeling:

- Anxious
- Uncomfortable
- Frustrated

TIGHT MOUTH

Visual signs:

- A closed mouth with lips forward
- Muzzle may appear puffed up
- Whiskers flare forward

What your dog may be feeling:

- Concerned
- Serious
- Annoyed

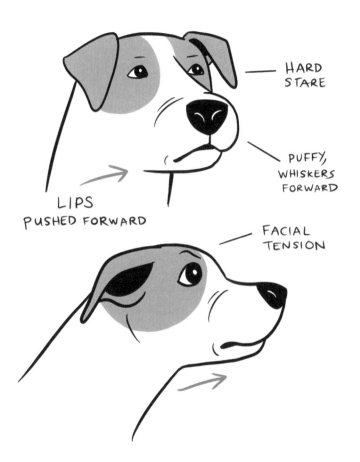

HARD STARE

PUFFY, WHISKERS FORWARD

LIPS PUSHED FORWARD

FACIAL TENSION

SNARLING MOUTH

Visual signs:

- Open mouth, top teeth showing
- Lips are forward in a C-shape pucker
- Face and body show tension

What your dog may be feeling:

- Very concerned or stressed
- Ready to fight
- If ears are forward, feeling confident (see p.82)
- If ears are pinned back, terrified (see p.84)

WRINKLED MUZZLE

GRRRR

TOP & BOTTOM TEETH SHOWING

LIPS FORWARD

BACK OFF!

"C-SHAPE" FORWARD MOUTH

MOUTHS

APPEASING GRIN

Often misinterpreted as "aggressive" or "happy".

Visual signs:

- Looks like a very wide grin
- Top and bottom teeth showing
- Posture is lowered

What your dog may be feeling:

- Friendly, but unconfident about this situation
- "Please, let's not fight!"

CONFLICTED OR STRESSED

These are signals that a dog is feeling uncomfortable about their situation.

LIP OR NOSE LICK

Visual signs:

- Quick licking of lip or nose when there is no food present

What your dog may be feeling:

- Concerned
- Uneasy
- Needing to reduce tension
- "Please take it easy."

STRESS YAWN

Visual signs:

- A short yawn
- Body is not relaxed or sleepy
- May include a squeaky wincing sound

What your dog may be feeling:

- Anxious
- Uneasy
- Needing to release tension
- Needing to avoid conflict
- "I need a break."

HEAD TURNING AWAY

(or offering one's back)

Often misinterpreted as "impolite" or "stubborn".

Visual signs:

- Turning head away or looking away from the source of stress

What your dog may be feeling:

- Uneasy
- Confused
- Needing to ease tension
- Wanting to politely interrupt an interaction
- "Excuse me a moment."

GROUND SNIFFING OR DIGGING

Visual signs:

- Suddenly sniffing the ground or digging when someone or something appears (there may be nothing on the ground)

What your dog may be feeling:

- Anxious
- Uncertain about the situation
- Needing to focus on something else
- Wanting to avoid interaction
- "This is too weird."
- "Don't mind me. I'm not interesting."

SCRATCHING OR LICKING

Like sniffing or digging, this is another example of a dog doing something out of context due to anxiety.

Visual signs:

- Suddenly scratching or licking themselves while in the middle of doing something else (when not really itchy)

What your dog may be feeling:

- Anxious
- Uncertain about the situation
- Needing to release tension
- Needing to focus on something else

SHAKING OFF

Visual signs:

- Shaking off when not wet

What your dog may be feeling:

- Stress release!
- Needing to calm down
- Shifting gears
- Shaking off is a release of stress and tension during or after an intense experience. It is also a polite way to interrupt a social interaction.
- "Excuse me, I need a moment."
- "Enough, thank you!"

ZOOMIES

Frequently misunderstood as "happy play!"

Visual signs:

- Suddenly running around really fast
- Rounded lower back, tucked tail
- May include bows and jumpy movements

What your dog may be feeling:

- Relief!
- Pressure release!
- Zoomies are a release of pent-up energy following a period of boredom, being restrained, a challenging experience or overexcitement.
- Puppies often get the Zoomies before doing a poop.

TUCKED
BUTT

FREEZING OR STILLNESS

(when not followed by playful movements)

Freezing is often mistaken for "calmness".

Visual signs:

- Closed mouth, held breath
- Body is still and tense
- Tail is stiff
- Not responsive, immovable

What your dog may be feeling:

- Concern
- Anxiety
- Fear
- Longer freezing or planting flat on the ground may indicate that the dog is so stressed that they have shut down.
- If freezing precedes Stalking (see p.38), the dog is feeling confident and focused.

PACING

Visual signs:

- Unable to relax or settle down

What your dog may be feeling:

- Very anxious
- Scared

Pacing may include other signs of stress:

- Drooling, panting, shedding, sweaty paws and whining

COWERING OR HIDING

Visual signs:

- Rounded spine or back with tucked tail
- Making the body as small as possible
- Can be standing or sitting

What your dog may be feeling:

- Very scared
- Very sad
- Cowering can go from slight to extreme. The more rounded and tucked-in the posture, the more stressed the dog is.

EARS

Ears are not only for hearing. A dog's ears can be flexible and expressive of how they are feeling.

RELAXED, NEUTRAL EARS

Visual signs:

- Soft, flexible ears
- How a neutral ear position looks will depend on the dog's breed and ear type.

What your dog may be feeling:

- Relaxed

ALERT EARS

Visual signs:

- Ears move up and rotate forward

What your dog may be feeling:

- Interested
- Attentive
- Excited

PINNED-BACK EARS

Visual signs:

- Ears are forced back flat against head
- In some floppy-eared dogs, the more stressed the dog is, the more "pinched" the ear flaps look.

What your dog may be feeling:

- Scared
- Anxious
- Sad

DROPPED EARS

(not to be confused with Pinned-Back Ears – see p.84)

Visual signs:

- Ears are moved down, sideways or back but not pressed against the head

What your dog may be feeling:

- If leaning away and avoiding someone, this is uncertainty or worry.
- If approaching someone with soft eyes, this is friendly and non-confrontational.

PLAY BODY LANGUAGE

Play is non-serious "ritualized conflict" and play body language can look like stress or aggression, with sudden brief freezes, wide-eyed stares (that look like "Whale Eye", see p.30), loud growling, biting and giant teeth displays.

We know that this is play when there are:

- Back-and-forth interactions
- Matched level of energy between dogs
- Easy, bouncy movements
- Space between mouths and bodies
- Biting without hurting
- Play breaks

PLAY!

FRIENDLY PLAY

More visual signs:

- When two dogs are playing, they may switch roles between being chaser and chased, top and bottom or biter and bitten: "predator" and "prey".

- Bigger dogs may roll over on the ground to make themselves smaller when playing with smaller dogs.

PLAY!

PLAY BOW

Visual signs:

- Elbows down on the ground and butt up!
- Wagging tail

What your dog may be feeling:

- Happy
- Excited
- Wanting attention
- "Are we playing?"
- "Are you coming?"

BUTT IS UP

HEAD AND CHEST ARE DOWN

ELBOWS ON THE GROUND

FRONT LEGS EXTENDED

PLAY FACES

Visual signs:

- Exaggerated "Whale Eye" (large eyes)
- Exaggerated open mouths with or without teeth
- Fake biting (no hurting)

What your dog may be feeling:

- Happy
- Having a blast!

Play faces can look like "aggression" or "anxiety" if seen out of context, but when dogs are playing these are happy faces!

REMEMBER:

Play is in danger of not being fun if one dog's stress signals are ignored by the other dog, or if there is intense interaction without play breaks.

MOUTH OPEN, LIPS PULLED BACK

BIG EYES

"C-SHAPE" MOUTH

"JAW SPARRING"

BIG EYES, EARS BACK

ROUNDED MOUTH, LIPS PULLED OVER TEETH

PLAY BREAKS

Visual signs:

- Short pauses, looking away
- Moving away from each other
- Shaking off
- Sniffing the ground
- Drinking water

What your dog may be feeling:

- Needing a break
- Taking a breath
- Recharge and refresh!

Play breaks are normal and healthy. Without these pauses, the excitement might escalate to stress and fighting.

TAILS

Here is a guide to looking at tail positions in relation to the whole body.

RELAXED, NEUTRAL TAIL

Visual signs:

- What a relaxed and neutral tail position looks like will depend on the dog breed and tail type.

What your dog may be feeling:

- Relaxed
- Happy

TIP:

Look at the butts. Relaxed tails are attached to relaxed butts.

TAIL FOLLOWS TOP LINE

GENTLE WAGS

NATURALLY HIGH TAIL

JUST HANGIN' OUT

NATURALLY LOW TAIL

ANXIOUS, LOW TAIL

Visual signs:

- Tail is clamped down over the butt or tucked under
- Some fluffy and curly dog tails may not fully unfurl or tuck but will still lower at the base.

What your dog may be feeling:

- Unsure
- Anxious
- Scared

The lower or more tucked-under the tail, the more anxious or fearful the dog is feeling.

CLAMPED
DOWN
OVER BUTT

LOWERED,
UNFURLED

TUCKED
UNDER

ALERT, HIGH TAIL

Visual signs:

- Tail is held high – loose or stiff
- Naturally high and curly tails may curl more tightly toward the dog's head.

What your dog may be feeling:

- Alert
- Excited or agitated, depending on other body language
- The more excited or agitated the dog feels, the higher the tail and the faster the wag.

DIFFERENT KINDS OF TAIL

- The tail alone does not tell the whole story, especially with dogs that have short or inflexible tails.
- Always look at the looseness or tightness of the dog's whole body within context.

NEUTRAL POSITION

PLAYFUL

ZZZZ

SLEEPY

ALERT, POINTING

LOWERED

TENTATIVE

NEUTRAL POSITION

RELAXED

NO TAIL

APPREHENSIVE

KNOW THE DIFFERENCE

Many similar-looking signals are often misinterpreted. Looking at the dog's whole body and the context is essential to interpretation.

WAGGING TAILS

Conventional wisdom says that a wagging tail means a dog is happy. This isn't always true. What is happening with the whole body?

HIGH WAGS

- If the face and body are tense, the dog is agitated. A stiff and narrow wag is NOT friendly.
- If the butt is wiggly, the dog is excited and playful.

HARD STARE,
TIGHT MOUTH

TIGHTLY
CURLED

STIFF,
NARROW
WAGS

WIGGLY,
LOOSE

KNOW THE DIFFERENCE

WIDE vs TIGHT WAGS

- If the strokes are broad, this is happiness.
- If the strokes are tight and there are stress signals, this is not a happy wag!

CIRCLE WAG OR "HELICOPTER TAIL"

- With body wiggles and wide fast circles, this is the happiest wag of all!

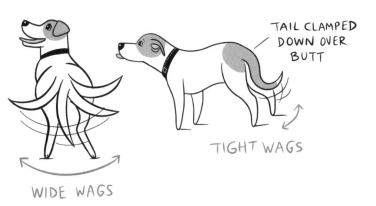

TAIL CLAMPED DOWN OVER BUTT

TIGHT WAGS

WIDE WAGS

"HELICOPTER TAIL"

WHEE!!!

EXPOSED BELLIES

This vulnerable posture is often misinterpreted as a belly-rub request.

"I AM NO THREAT. PLEASE STOP."

- If a dog is lying on their side, with a tense and straight body, they are feeling unsure and worried.

UPSIDE-DOWN PLAY

- If a dog is rolling around, back flat on the ground, body loose and wiggly, they are feeling trusting and playful.

TIP:

Most dogs prefer having their upper bodies petted, not their bellies!

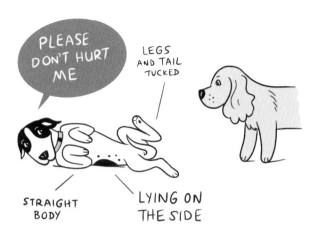

KISSES

Dog licks are often misinterpreted as wanting affection. You need to look at the whole body and interaction to get the full picture.

AFFECTIONATE KISSES

- If a dog approaches with soft eyes and soft licks, you either taste delicious or they want to be close to you.

DISMISSING KISSES

- If a dog offers pushy licks, while their bodies show tension and conflicted signals, they are feeling anxious and you may be too close for comfort.

- "You can go now."

KNOW THE DIFFERENCE

PAW LIFT

One lifted paw – be it a small or large movement – can have many different interpretations . Here are just a few.

UNCERTAINTY, FEAR

- If there are other signs of anxiety, the dog may be feeling confused or scared.

ANTICIPATION

- If the whole body is alert, this paw lift signals curiosity and expectation.

"PLAY WITH ME!"

- If a paw lift is accompanied by a head tilt and bouncy movements, this is most likely an invitation to play!

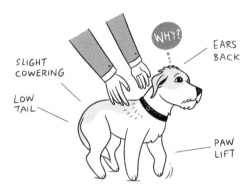

KNOW THE DIFFERENCE

CALM

Is it really calmness or is it extreme fear?

RELAXED CALMNESS

- If a dog's face and body are relaxed and they are able to move around easily and do different things, they are calm and not concerned about anything in particular.

SHUT DOWN

- If the dog is planted down, keeping very still or moving with unusual slowness, they may feel totally powerless or frozen in fear. This is not a healthy emotional state.

PANTING

"I AM HOT"

- If there are no stress signals, a dog is panting to cool down or to get more air.

STRESS PANTING

- If there is facial and body tension, this is anxiety. Stress panting can sound dry and raspy.

"LAUGHING"

- If the tongue stays in the mouth, and the breathy panting stops and starts in response to play interaction, this dog is having fun!

SOFT EYES

PANT PANT PANT

RELAXED BODY

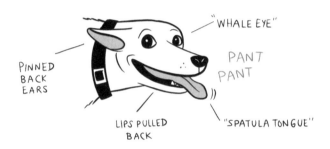

"WHALE EYE"

PINNED BACK EARS

PANT PANT

LIPS PULLED BACK

"SPATULA TONGUE"

SOFT EYES

PANT PANT PANT PANT

PLAYFUL MOVEMENTS

SNIFFING THE GROUND

What is the context?

INVESTIGATING OR EXPLORING

- If in a smelly location, a dog may sniff the ground to get more information, forage for food or seek out particular scents. This is fun, interesting and important for them to do.

EASING TENSION

- If in the middle of a challenging or strange situation, a dog may sniff the ground to politely avoid interaction and calm themselves down.

CONGRATULATIONS!

You have now taken the first steps to understanding doggie language.

To continue your journey, pay attention to your best friend in different situations, and let them guide you to a better understanding of what stresses them, what excites them and what makes them happy!

DOGGIELANGUAGEBOOK.com

THANK YOU

I have learned from so many experts over the years that I can't possibly list all their names here. I am very grateful to these inspiring dog behaviour educators and authors for helping me with this book.

Marjie Alonso

Eileen Anderson

Dr Sarah-Elizabeth Byosiere

Dr Amy Cook

Linda Lombardi

Sassafras Lowrey

Jennifer Shryock

Kellie Sisson Snider

Patricia Tirrell

Dr Zazie Todd

Mara Velez

Thank you also to my literary agent Lilly Ghahremani, and to my editors Claire Plimmer and Debbie Chapman for believing in me!

If you're interested in finding out more
about our books, find us on Facebook
at Summersdale Publishers and follow us
on Twitter at @Summersdale.

Thanks very much for buying
this Summersdale book.

www.summersdale.com